Security Arabic

Books in the series

Media Persian
Dominic Parviz Brookshaw

Internet Arabic
Mourad Diouri

Security Arabic
Mark Evans

Media Arabic
2nd edition
Elisabeth Kendall

www.euppublishing.com/series/emev

• Essential Middle Eastern Vocabularies •

Security Arabic

Mark Evans

EDINBURGH
University Press

© Mark Evans, 2013

Edinburgh University Press Ltd
22 George Square, Edinburgh
www.euppublishing.com

Typeset in Times New Roman and
printed and bound in Great Britain by
CPI Group (UK) Ltd, Croydon CR0 4YY

A CIP record for this book is available from the
British Library

ISBN 978 0 7486 4661 6 (paperback)
ISBN 978 0 7486 4663 0 (webready PDF)
ISBN 978 0 7486 4966 2 (epub)
ISBN 978 0 7486 4965 5 (Amazon ebook)

The right of Mark Evans to be identified as author
of this work has been asserted in accordance with
the Copyright, Designs and Patents Act 1988.

The e-Learning materials (audio recording and
e-Flashcard sets) were produced by Mourad Diouri
(e-Learning Lecturer/Developer in Arabic Studies,
University of Edinburgh).

Published with the support of the Edinburgh
University Scholarly Publishing Initiatives Fund.

CONTENTS

User Guide	vi
Introduction	1
1. General	5
2. Global Security	13
3. Organisations	23
4. Energy Security	27
5. Weapons of Mass Destruction (WMD)	31
6. Defence & Military	39
7. Law Enforcement	45
8. Counter Terrorism	51
9. Human Intelligence	57
10. Communications Technology	63
11. Information Technology	69
12. Information Security	73
13. Intelligence Analysis	81
Index	85

USER GUIDE

To enhance your ability to recall the vocabulary and to pronounce it correctly, this book is accompanied by audio recordings and audio-visual e-Flashcards of the entire contents of each chapter, recorded in both English and Arabic. This e-Learning material is provided in two formats: 1. Audio recordings compatible with iPods and other devices (via MP3 files on the CD accompanying this book and via http://www.euppublishing.com/page/emev/e-learning); 2. Audio-visual e-Flashcards (via http://www.euppublishing.com/page/emev/e-learning). Material on the website requires access token 46616Eva.

Audio recordings

Main features
- Each Arabic term is recorded with authentic native pronunciation at normal speed.
- Each Arabic term is preceded by its equivalent in English.
- Each chapter is recorded as a single MP3 track (the track numbers correspond to the chapter numbers, e.g. Track 01 = Chapter 1).
- The audio files can be played on a computer or transferred to an MP3 device (e.g. iPod, mobile phone, etc.), enabling you to study on the move.

Tips
- Make sure that you engage actively with the audio recordings by repeating each Arabic term during the pause.

- Pause the recording and challenge yourself to produce the Arabic word before it is announced.

Audio-visual e-Flashcards

Main features
- Designed with the language-learning software Before You Know It (BYKI), available as a free download suitable for Windows or Mac at www.byki.com/fls (select 'Arabic' as your chosen language).
- Each e-Flashcard contains the English term on one side and the Arabic on the reverse.
- Each Arabic term is recorded with authentic native pronunciation.
- The native speaker sound can be slowed down for paced listening.
- Vocabulary acquisition is accelerated through a variety of fun interactive self-assessment activities.

Tips
Keep track of your progress through BYKI's interactive self-assessment modes:
- Preview it: learn and review the vocabulary in e-Flashcard mode including audio, without being assessed.
- Recognise it: test your recognition of the vocabulary in English from the Arabic side, and vice versa.
- Produce it: test your knowledge of the vocabulary in English by typing its translation in Arabic, and vice versa.

Download

The *Security Arabic* BYKI sets are available at http://www.euppublishing.com/page/emev/e-learning using access code 46616Eva. For more information about BYKI, go to www.byki.com.

INTRODUCTION

Middle East security issues remain prominent in the Arab, Western and wider media, and are followed closely by public and private sector organisations worldwide, in areas of foreign policy, international cooperation and development, defence and academia. Arabic security terminology is constantly evolving, as new words and terms are coined and new concepts integrated. This 'quick-fix' vocabulary of security and intelligence Arabic is essential to students of Arabic, primarily at intermediate and advanced levels, and to individuals or organisations engaging with the Arab world.

As part of the *Essential Middle Eastern Vocabularies* series, this book aims to provide the core Arabic vocabulary for the topics of security and intelligence, to facilitate easy learning, reference and translation of terminology between Arabic and English. The book will prove indispensable for anyone developing or using Arabic skills in these and other subject areas, whether for discussion, interpreting, reading, translation, listening comprehension or for interacting with Arabic speakers or Arab TV, radio or internet sources.

The book comprises thirteen chapters covering primary security and intelligence topics: General; Global Security; Organisations; Energy Security; Weapons of Mass Destruction (WMD); Defence & Military; Law Enforcement; Counter Terrorism; Human Intelligence; Communications Technology; Information Technology; Information Security; Intelligence Analysis. The vocabulary featured here is not exhaustive. It is derived from internet and other research on current usage and from files and databases developed in support of training and language work, built from on-the-job experience in the relevant fields. Every effort has been made to place terminology in the most appropriate chapter and to avoid repetition as far as possible. Instead of relying upon alphabetical lists, chapters are arranged to follow an internal logic which aids learning within a conceptual and/or linguistic framework. An alphabetised English index is provided at the end of the book for convenient reference.

Notes on the formal presentation

Vowelling has not been included, except in First Form verbs. These are supplied in the form of the basic stem (past tense masculine singular, with the middle vowel marked where it is not a fatha) followed by the present tense (masculine singular), with the masdar given in brackets. Shadda has been omitted on a final 'ya' where it simply indicates a nisba adjective. Guidance on pronunciation is provided by the accompanying CD and the audio-visual e-Flashcards, available online.

Nouns are generally presented in the indefinite form, but the definite article is used to reflect common usage with generic concepts and compound nouns. Noun plurals have been included (separated from the singular by a comma) only where these are commonly found in use and not easy to predict.

I would like to thank Lis Kendall for her support and insights during the preparation of this book.

Thanks also to Mourad Diouri for his contributions on audio-visual materials and editing, and to Edinburgh University Press for their advice and work on production. I hope you find this publication of interest and use in developing your own acquaintance with this challenging and rewarding language.

Mark Evans

1. GENERAL

أمن قومي	national security
تهديد للأمن القومي	national security threat
أمن جماعي	collective security
دراسات أمنية	security studies
أمن مادي	physical security
درع أمني	security shield
متطلّبات الأمن	security requirements
أوّلية	priority
اكتشاف ومنع الجرائم الأشدّ خطورة	detection and prevention of serious crime
سلامة اقتصادية	economic wellbeing
استقرار اقتصادي	economic stability
استقرار النظام	regime stability
حماية البيئة	environmental protection
مخابرات	intelligence (organisation)

استخبارات	intelligence (e.g. reports)
جمع يجمَع معلومات استخبارية (جَمْع)	to gather intelligence
استخبارات العمليات	operational intelligence
استخبارات جوّية استراتيجية	strategic air intelligence
تحفّظي	preventive
أمان	safety
دفاع مدني	civil defence
خطّة طوارئ	emergency plan
أعلن حالة الطوارئ	to declare a state of emergency
عملية إخلاء اضطرارية	emergency evacuation
تعطّل	malfunction
في حالة إنذار تامّ	on full alert
حالة استنفار	alert status
حالة تأهّب	"
حالة التهديد	threat state

تهديد بالقوّة	threat of force
تهديد فوري	immediate threat
شكّل تهديداً	to constitute a threat
تخفيض التهديد	threat reduction
إخطار عاجل	short notice
حسّاس بالزمن	time-critical
مرحلة حرجة	critical phase
موقف حرج	critical situation
وضع أمني	security situation
موقف مستقرّ	stabilised situation
غرفة عمليات	situation room
التحكّم الأرضي	ground control
قنوات الاتّصال	communication channels
مركز الاتّصالات	communications centre
قنوات التقارير	reporting channels
الجهات المختصّة	the relevant authorities

8 • GENERAL

منطقة المسؤوليات	area of responsibility
رئيس المحطّة	station chief
محطّة خارجية	outstation
فرعية	"
فريق عمل	task force
قوّة مشتركة	joint task force
فريق تفكير	think tank
عقلية	mindset
فريق منعقد عن بعد	virtual team
أسلوب متعدّد التخصّصات	multi-disciplinary approach
متعدّد الأغراض	multi-purpose
شغّل	to activate/initialise
شغّل جهاز الإنذار	to activate the alarm
كاميرا مخفية	concealed camera
تلفزيون دائرة مغلقة	closed circuit television (CCTV)
آلة تصوير نبضية سينية	X-ray pulse camera

متحذِّر من الأمن	security-conscious
فرض يفرِض الأمن (فَرْض)	to enforce security
إجراءات أمنية مشدّدة	heightened security measures/procedures
تدابير أمن مضادّة	security counter measures
التزام بالإجراءات	compliance with procedure
سياسة أمنية عامّة	corporate security policy
اختراق أمني	security breach
موادّ محظورة	prohibited items/materials
منطقة محظورة	prohibited zone
منطقة ممنوعة	restricted area
معلومات مقصورة	restricted information
قسَّم	to compartment (e.g. information)
على مبدأ الحاجة إلى المعرفة	on a need-to-know basis
تناسب	proportionality
مسؤولية	accountability

شفَافية	transparency
حماية البيانات	data protection
تداول المعلومات السرّية	handling of confidential information
سرّية	confidentiality
تصريح أمني	security clearance
تدقيق متطوّر	developed vetting (DV)
تصنيف السرّية	protective marking/ security classification
خريطة تصنيف	classification chart
سرّي	secret
سرّي للغاية	top secret
وثائق رسمية	official documents
وثائق مصنّفة	classified documents
وثائق غير مصنّفة	unclassified documents
فرع الوثائق الفنّية	technical documents branch
وثائق السفر	travel documents
حفِظ يحفَظ ورقة، أوراق (حِفْظ)	to guard a document

كاشف الأسرار	whistle blower
ملفّ أمني	security dossier/file
مزّق \ قطّع	to shred (paper)
آلة تقطيع الأوراق	paper shredder

2. GLOBAL SECURITY

الأمن العالمي	global security
تكامل أمني	security integration
مبادرة دفاع تعاوني	cooperative defence initiative
حزام أمني	security belt
قوّات الأمن	security forces
أهمّية استراتيجية	strategic importance
الدول العظمى	superpowers
قاعدة السلطة	power base
دول المحور	axis powers
محور الشرّ	axis of evil
المنافسة في الحرب الباردة	Cold War rivalry
قنوات دبلوماسية	diplomatic channels
ضابط اتّصال	liaison officer
قطع يقطَع العلاقات الدبلوماسية (قَطْع)	to sever diplomatic relations
حصانة دبلوماسية	diplomatic immunity

حقيبة دبلوماسية	diplomatic bag
نصيحة السفر	travel advice
شرطة الحدود	border police
مراقبة الحدود	border control
قوّات أمن الحدود	border security forces
حرس الحدود	Border Guard
جمرك، جمارك	customs
رقابة جمركية	customs control
بوّابة	checkpoint
فحص المسافرين	passenger screening
وكيل فاحص	screener/screening officer
ماسحة	scanner
مسح العين	eye scan
قياس حيوي	biometrics
طبع الأصابع	fingerprinting
مخدّرات	narcotics
مكافحة المخدّرات	counter narcotics
تهريب المخدّرات	drug trafficking

تاجر مخدّرات، تجّار مخدّرات	drug dealer
الهيئة الدولية لمراقبة المخدّرات	international narcotics control board
عملية حدودية	cross-border operation
الجريمة المنظّمة عبر الحدود الوطنية	transnational organised crime
شحنة محظورة	illicit cargo
شحنة عالية الاهتمام	high-interest cargo
تهريب الأسلحة	weapons smuggling
هجرة غير شرعية	illegal immigration
مهاجر غير شرعي	illegal immigrant
تهريب البشر	human trafficking
ملتمس اللجوء	asylum seeker
استرداد	extradition
تسليم	"
تسليم استثنائي	extraordinary rendition
جريمة تستوجب تسليم مرتكبها	extraditable offence
قاوم التسليم	to fight extradition

سلّم	to hand over (e.g. for extradition)
معاهدة تسليم	extradition treaty
الاتّفاقية الأوروبّية المتعلّقة بتسليم المجرمين	European convention on extradition
أحال نزاعاً إلى المحكمة الدولية	to refer a dispute to the international court
نظام عقوبات	sanctions regime
قوّات حفظ السلام	peacekeeping forces
منطقة الحظر الجوّي	no-fly zone
حرّيات مدنية	civil liberties
حقوق الانسان	human rights
قانون حقوق الانسان	Human Rights Act
ناشط حقوق الانسان	human rights activist
أزمة انسانية	humanitarian crisis
جرائم مرتكبة ضدّ الانسانية	crimes against humanity
جرائم حرب	war crimes
ارتكب إبادة جماعية	to commit genocide
تطهير عرقي	ethnic cleansing

انتهاك خطير	gross violation
حكم القانون	rule of law
فوضوية	anarchy
فوضى سياسية	political anarchy
ناشط سياسي	political activist
اتّبع مذهباً	to follow a doctrine
عقيدية، عقائد	dogma
عقيدية \ عقائدية	dogmatism
الإسلام السياسي	political Islam
أصولية	fundamentalism
أصولي	fundamentalist
جذرية \ راديكالية	radicalism
جذري \ راديكالي	radical
تطرّف \ تطرّفية	extremism
متطرّف	extremist
نازي جديد	neo-Nazi
منظّمة يمينية	right-wing organisation
معاداة السامية	anti-semitism

صهيونية	Zionism
صهيوني	Zionist
عنصرية	racism
عنصري	racist
طائفة أقلّية	minority faction
أغلبية \ أقلّية سنّية \ شيعية	Sunni/Shi'a majority/minority
حكم أقلّية	minority rule
أقلّية عنصرية	ethnic minority
كافر، كفّار	infidel
قبلية	tribalism
قومية عربية	Arab nationalism
حكومة وحدة وطنية	national unity government
الحرس الوطني	National Guard
طائفية	sectarianism
شمولية	totalitarianism
استبدادية	authoritarianism
فرض يفرِض السلطة (فَرْض)	to impose authority

تجاوز السلطة	to exceed/abuse (one's authority)
حكم عرفي	martial law
حظر التجوّل	curfew
دولة شرطة	police state
قمع	crackdown/repression
تضييق أمني	security clampdown
حكومة مطلقة \ أوتوقراطية	autocracy
دكتاتورية	dictatorship
عبادة الشخص	cult of personality
استعمارية	colonialism
محمية	protectorate
تغيير في النظام	regime change
تداول السلطة	transfer of power
سلطة ائتلاف مؤقّتة	coalition provisional authority
حكومة مؤقّتة	interim/caretaker government
تغيير مؤسّسي	institutional change
رجعي	reactionary

دمقرطة	democratisation
انتخابات حرّة ونزيهة	free and fair elections
مركز اقتراع	polling station
التحكّم في المضايق	control of the straits
مضيق هرمز	Strait of Hormuz
مضيق جبل طارق	Straits of Gibraltar
أزمة السويس	Suez crisis
عملية السلام في الشرق الأوسط	Middle East Peace Process (MEPP)
مرتفعات الجولان	Golan Heights
الضفّة الغربية	West Bank
الأراضي المحتلّة	the Occupied Territories
احتلال	occupation
غزوة	incursion
لاجئ سياسي	political refugee
إعادة توطين اللاجئين	refugee resettlement
تجميد بناء المستوطنات	freeze on settlements
إعادة البناء	reconstruction

GLOBAL SECURITY • 21

إجراءات بناء الثقة	confidence-building measures
معايير مزدوجة	double standards
عفو عامّ	general amnesty
أبعد من السياسة	to depoliticise
أسرة حاكمة	ruling family
ملكية دستورية	constitutional monarchy
القانون الدستوري	constitutional law
أسقط النظام	to overthrow the regime
انقلاب	coup/coup d'état/upheaval
حرب أهلية	civil war
ثورة	revolution
نهضة	uprising
انتفاضة	uprising/(Palestinian) intifada
الربيع العربي	Arab Spring
معارض	oppositionist
مخالف	dissenter

متظاهر	protester
انشقاقي	secessionist
انفصالي	separatist
مقاومة	resistance
صمود	resistance/staying power
حالة الطوارئ	state of emergency
تغيّر ديموغرافي	demographic change
انفجار سكّاني	demographic explosion
بطالة جماعية	mass unemployment

3. ORGANISATIONS

مجلس الأمن التابع للأمم المتّحدة	United Nations Security Council (UNSC)
الجمعية العامّة التابعة للأمم المتّحدة	UN General Assembly (UNGA)
الميثاق الأممي	UN Charter
مبادئ ميثاق الأمم المتّحدة	principles of the UN Charter
قرار مجلس الأمن التابع للأمم المتّحدة	UN Security Council Resolution (UNSCR)
اللجنة الخاصّة للأمم المتّحدة	UN Special Commission (UNSCOM)
قوّات الأمم المتّحدة المؤقّتة	UN Interim Force
وكالة إغاثة اللاجئين للأمم المتّحدة (الأنروا)	UN Relief and Works Agency (UNRWA)
منظّمة الأمم المتّحدة للتربية والعلوم والثقافة (اليونسكو)	UN Educational, Scientific and Cultural Organization (UNESCO)
بعثة الأمم المتّحدة	UN mission
مراقبو الأمم المتّحدة	UN observers

الوكالة الدولية للطاقة الذرّية	International Atomic Energy Agency (IAEA)
مجلس الأمن القومي	National Security Council
مستشار الأمن القومي	National Security Advisor
لجنة المخابرات التابعة لمجلس النوّاب	House Intelligence Committee
لجنة المخابرات التابعة لمجلس الشيوخ	Senate Intelligence Committee
لجنة المخابرات المشتركة	Joint Intelligence Committee
أجهزة المخابرات	intelligence apparatus
جماعة المخابرات \ مجموعة المخابرات	the intelligence community (IC)
مديرية الاستخبارات	intelligence directorate
وزارة الاستخبارات	Ministry of Intelligence
الداخلية \ وزارة الداخلية	Ministry of the Interior
وزارة الإعلام	Ministry of Information

bureau of investigation	مكتب مباحث
to call in the Federal Bureau of Investigation (FBI)	استدعى مكتب التحقيقات الفيدرالي
Central Intelligence Agency (CIA)	وكالة المخابرات المركزية
Arab League	جامعة الدول العربية
Arab League General Secretariat	الأمانة العامّة للجامعة العربية
Secretary General	أمين عامّ
Organization of the Islamic Conference (OIC)	منظّمة المؤتمر الإسلامي
Gulf Cooperation Council (GCC)	مجلس التعاون الخليجي
Palestine Liberation Organization (PLO)	منظّمة التحرير الفلسطينية
Muslim Brotherhood	الإخوان المسلمون
Islamic Salvation Front	جبهة الإنقاذ الإسلامي
Red Crescent	الهلال الأحمر

منظّمة العفو الدولية	Amnesty International
محكمة العدل الدولية	International Court of Justice (ICJ)
محكمة العدل الأوروبّية	European Court of Justice
المحكمة الجنائية الدولية	International Criminal Court (ICC)
ميثاق جنيف \ فيينا	Geneva/Vienna Convention
معاهدة روما	Rome Treaty
منظّمة حلف شمال الأطلسي	North Atlantic Treaty Organization (NATO)
وكالة تحديد الأسلحة ونزع السلاح	Arms Control and Disarmament Agency
الاتّحاد الأوروبّي	European Union (EU)
رابطة أمم جنوب شرق آسيا (الأسيان)	Association of South-East Asian Nations (ASEAN)
منظّمة الوحدة الإفريقية	Organization of African Unity (OAU)

4. ENERGY SECURITY

البنية التحتية القومية الحرجة	Critical National Infrastructure
منشأة حيوية	vital installation
شبكة الطاقة الكهربائية	power grid
محطّة توليد الكهرباء	power station
طاقة	energy
استهلاك	energy consumption
بقاء الطاقة	energy conservation
كفاية الطاقة	energy efficiency
الطاقة المتاحة	available energy
مصادر تقليدية للطاقة	conventional energy sources
طاقة من المناطق البحرية	offshore energy
طاقة بديلة	alternative energy
تنويع اقتصادي	economic diversification
تجهيز	supply
موارد	resources

ثروة نفطية	oil wealth
ثروة بترولية	"
حقول نفطية	oil fields
احتياطات النفط المحقّقة	proven oil reserves
تنقّب عن النفط	to explore for oil
تنقيب	exploration (oil)
بئر نفط، آبار نفط	oil well
نفط خام	crude oil
مصفاة نفط، مصافي نفط	oil refinery
تكرير النفط	oil refining
إنتاج النفط	oil production
منظّمة البلدان المصدّرة للنفط (أوبك \ الأوبك)	Organization of the Petroleum Exporting Countries (OPEC)
جمّد أسعار النفط	to freeze oil prices
تغيّر مناخي	climate change
مكافحة تغيّر المناخ	combating climate change
تنمية مستدامة	sustainable development

كارثة بيئية	environmental disaster
نقص المياه	water shortage
اتّفاق مياه النيل	Nile water agreement

5. WEAPONS OF MASS DESTRUCTION (WMD)

أسلحة الدمار الشامل	weapons of mass destruction (WMD)
نزع السلاح	disarmament
الحدّ من الأسلحة	arms control
سباق التسلّح	arms race
مبادرة دفاع استراتيجي	Strategic Defence Initiative
منظومة دفاعية مضادّة للقذائف الباليستية	ballistic missile defence system
الدفاع النووي البيولوجي الكيميائي	nuclear-biological-chemical defence
انتشار الأسلحة النووية	nuclear proliferation
مكافحة الانتشار	counter proliferation
صناعة الطاقة النووية	nuclear power industry
خزن يخزُن (خَزْن)	to stockpile
مخزون نووي احتياطي	nuclear stockpile
رادع نووي	nuclear deterrent

قوّات رادعة	deterrent forces
منطقة خالية من الأسلحة النووية	nuclear-free zone
معاهدة عدم انتشار الأسلحة النووية	nuclear non-proliferation treaty
معاهدة حظر التجارب الشامل	comprehensive test-ban treaty
تخفيض تدريجي	step-by-step reduction
نظام مراقبة تكنولوجيا القذائف	Missile Technology Control Regime
معلومات متحكّم في تصديرها	export controlled information
موادّ خاضعة للمراقبة	controlled substances
نقل الأسلحة	weapons transfer
نقل التكنولوجيا	technology transfer
سلسلة تموين	supply chain
طريق تموين رئيسي	main supply route
ضمانات الوكالة الدولية للطاقة الذرّية	IAEA safeguards
نظام مراقبة، أنظمة مراقبة	monitoring system
نظام التفتيش	inspections regime

فتّش	to inspect
مفتّش أسلحة	arms inspector
قياس عن بعد	telemetry
محسّس عن بعد	remote sensor
تحكّم عن بعد	remote control
دفاع الفضاء	aerospace defence
قذفيات	ballistics
صاروخ بالستي عابر للقارّات	inter-continental ballistic missile
صاروخ بالستي قصير المدى	short-range ballistic missile
عربة الرجوع	re-entry vehicle
منظومة التوجيه	guidance system
وقود سائل لدفع القذائف	liquid missile propellant
وقود جافّ	solid fuel
حمولة	payload
رأس حربي	warhead
رأس حربي نووي حراري	thermo-nuclear warhead

nuclear fission	اندماج نووي
fissile material	مادّة انشطارية
atomic mass	كتلة ذرّية
depleted uranium	يورانيوم منضّب
centrifuge	جهاز الطرد المركزي، أجهزة الطرد المركزية
highly enriched uranium	يورانيوم مخصّب جدّاً
isotope separation	فصل نظائري
revolutions per minute (rpm)	دورات في الدقيقة
radiation detection instrument	أداة كشف الإشعاع
radiation protection instruments	أدوات للوقاية من الإشعاع
protective action	أعمال وقائية
preventive action	أعمال مانعة
radiological release	إطلاق إشعاعي
radiological protection	حماية إشعاعية
radiological warfare	حرب إشعاعية

تخريب إشعاعي	radiological sabotage
مرض إشعاعي	radiation sickness
سيناريو أسوأ الأحوال	worst-case scenario
منطقة تهديد عالٍ	high threat area
تفاعل متسلسل	chain reaction
تفاعل نووي	nuclear reaction
مفاعل نووي	nuclear reactor
جهاز نووي	nuclear device
حادث انصهار قلب المفاعل	reactor core meltdown
مقياس ريختر	Richter scale
موجة اهتزاز	shock wave
شعاع جيمي، أشعّة جيمية	gamma ray
تعرّض مباشر	direct exposure
جرعة إشعاعية حادّة	acute radiation dose
سقاطة إشعاعية	radioactive fallout
إشعاع خلفي	background radiation
انحلال إشعاعي	radioactive decay
عمر النصف الإشعاعي	radioactive half-life

تطهير إشعاعي	radioactive decontamination
تطهير طارئ	emergency decontamination
نقل النفايات الخطيرة	transport of hazardous waste
إزالة التلوّث	cleanup
أنهى الخدمة نهائياً	to decommission
جزيء، جزيئات	particle
سلاح شعاع جزيئات	particle beam weapon
سلاح نشر الإشعاع	radiation dispersal weapon
انقشاع	dispersion
جهاز احتواء	containment device
منظومة استطلاع بيولوجي	biological reconnaissance system
برنامج دفاع بيولوجي	biological defence programme
بكتيريا	bacteria
طاعون	plague
حرب جرثومية	germ warfare

عامل الأعصاب، عوامل الأعصاب	nerve agent
عامل شلّ القدرة	incapacitating agent
عامل فقاعي	blister agent
غاز الخردل	mustard gas
كاشف الغاز	gas detector
قناع الغاز	gas mask
بدلة وقاية	protective suit
تقنية البقاء حيّاً	survival technology
ملجأ حماية	protection shelter

6. DEFENCE & MILITARY

قيادة وسيطرة	command and control (C2)
مركز قيادة وسيطرة	command and control centre
سلسلة القيادة	chain of command
رئيس أركان القوّات المسلّحة	Armed Forces Chief of Staff
رئيس أركان العمليات	Chief of Staff, Operations
تمارين عسكرية	military exercises/manoeuvres
استخدام القوّة	use of force
مضاعف القوّة	force multiplier
صراع مسلّح	armed conflict
ترسانة	arsenal
تكنولوجيا دفاعية	defence technology
قوّات تحالف	coalition forces
فيلق الردّ السريع المقدّم	Advanced Rapid Reaction Corps (ARRC)

مغوار، مغاوير	commando
قوّات خاصّة	special forces
قوّات العاصفة	storm troops
اقتحم	to storm
شنّ يشُنّ عملية (شَنّ)	to launch/mount an operation
عملية سرِّية	covert operation
إجراء التشغيل القياسي	standard operating procedure
حالة الاستعداد	readiness status
الاستعدادية القتالية	combat readiness
التأهّب التشغيلي	operational readiness
حرب نفسية	psychological warfare
حرب إلكترونية	electronic warfare
نبض كهرمغنطيسي	electromagnetic pulse
ليزر	laser
مكشاف الأشعّة دون الحمراء	infra-red detector
قصف بموجات متناهية الصغر	microwave bombardment

طائرة بدون طيّار	unmanned aerial vehicle (UAV)/ drone
منظومة جوّية للإنذار والمراقبة	airborne warning and control system (AWACS)
طائرة أواكس	AWACS aircraft
استطلاع	reconnaissance
استطلاع جوّي	aerial reconnaissance
طائرة استطلاع	reconnaissance aircraft
طائرة مراقبة	surveillance aircraft
طائرة استكشاف بحرية	navy reconnaissance plane
استطلاع بالأقمار الصناعية	satellite reconnaissance
استطلاع تصويري	photographic reconnaissance
منظومة مراقبة	surveillance system
رصيف مراقبة، أرصفة مراقبة	surveillance platform
سونار إيجابي \ سلبي	active/passive sonar
نظام الملاحة	navigation system

جهاز توجيه	homing device/beacon
منظومة التعريف	identification system
تمييز	identification friend or foe (IFF)
تغطية رادارية	radar coverage
رادار الإنذار المبكّر	early warning radar
رادار قيادة النيران	fire control radar
رادار مشعّ	illumination radar
مقطع عرضي راداري	radar cross section
مسافة احتياز	acquisition range
أطبق على هدف	to lock onto a target
أسلحة ذكية	smart weapons
قصف دقيق	precision bombing
صاروخ كروز مطلق جوّياً	air-launched cruise missile
تقدير أضرار المعارك	battle damage assessment (BDA)
تقرير موقف	situation report (sitrep)
إدراك موقعي	situational awareness

observation post	مركز مراقبة \ مرصد
no man's land/neutral territory	منطقة حرام \ أراضي حرام
buffer zone	منطقة عازلة
"	منطقة فاصلة
electronic counter measures	إجراءات مضادّة للإلكترونيات
chaff rockets	صواريخ عاكسة للرادار

7. LAW ENFORCEMENT

وكالة إنفاذ القانون	law enforcement agency
قوّات إنفاذ القانون	law enforcement forces
حفِظ يحفَظ القانون والنظام (حِفْظ)	to maintain law and order
الضوابط والتوازنات	checks and balances
سند توكيل	power of attorney
شرطة المدينة	metropolitan police
شرطة عسكرية	military police
نقطة بوليس	police post
أعاق عمل الشرطة	to obstruct the police
رئيس شرطة	police chief
شرطي \ ضابط شرطة	police officer
شرطة خيّالة	mounted police
شرطة هجّانة	(camel) mounted police
شرطة الانترنت	internet police

بصّاص	detective
محقّق شرطة	police investigator
تحقيق مستقلّ	independent investigation
سلطات تحقيقية	investigatory powers
بدأ يبدَأ تحقيقاً جنائياً (بَدْء)	to launch a criminal investigation
بحث يبحَث (بَحْث)	to investigate
تحقيق	investigation
يُرجى التحرّي (عن)	investigation is requested (into)
استنطق	to interrogate/question
استدلال	fact-finding
حقن يحقِن المعلومات (حَقْن)	to withhold information
فحص يفحَص (فَحْص)	to check (up on)
تابع	to follow up
متابعة	follow up/pursuit
قائمة مراجعة	check list
مستندات	supporting documents

دليل، أدلّة \ دلائل	lead/clue/evidence
مشبوه	under suspicion/suspect
غير مشبوه	not under suspicion (clean)
أنشطة محظورة	prohibited activities
تحقيق في غسل الأموال	money-laundering investigation
فرقة مكافحة الاحتيال	fraud squad
وثائق مزيّفة	forged documents
وثائق أصلية	authentic documents
رشوة	bribery/bribe
تعقّب	to track/trace/run a trace/tail
أمر محكمة، أوامر محكمة	warrant
أمر قبض	arrest warrant
أمر تفتيش	search warrant
نفّذ أمر محكمة	to serve a warrant
محتجز	detained
في الحبس	in custody

أخذ يأخُذ للمحكمة (أَخْذ)	to take to court
محكمة تحقيق	court of inquiry
محكمة عسكرية	court martial/ military court
محكمة استئناف	appeal court
ارتكب جرماً	to commit an offence
اتّهم بجرم جنائي	to charge with a criminal offence
اتّهام	indictment
محاكمة	trial/hearing
أمام القضاء	on trial
بانتظار المحاكمة	on remand
مركز حجز	remand centre
وضع تحت كفالة	to remand on bail
نكل ينكِل عن الكفالة (نُكول)	to jump bail
أطلق سراحه بكفالة	he was released on bail
تحت الاختبار	on probation
فترة الاختبار	probation period
غرامة	fine

غرّم	to fine/impose a fine
معسكر اعتقال	detention centre
اعتقال وقائي	protective custody
أوقف	to remand in custody
حبس احتياطي	provisional detention
حكم بالسجن مدى الحياة	life prison sentence
زنزانة	prison cell
حرس مسلّح	armed guard
مظاهرات	demonstrations
شغب	riot
اضطرابات	riots/disturbances
حرّض	to incite
فتنة	sedition
شرطة منع الشغب	riot police
عامل مكافحة الشغب	riot control agent
معدّات مكافحة الشغب	riot gear
بزّة مضادّة للرصاص	body armour
هراوة	baton/truncheon
غاز مسيّل للدموع	tear gas

قنبلة مسيّلة للدموع	tear gas grenade
قنبلة تخدير	stun grenade
بندقية تخدير	stun gun
قنبلة دخان	smoke bomb
أصفاد \ كلبشة	handcuffs
قميص كتاف	strait jacket
سلاح ناري	firearm
خرطوم مياه	water cannon
طوّق منطقة	to cordon off an area
حزام \ كوردون	cordon

8. COUNTER TERRORISM

الحرب على الإرهاب	war on terror
مكافحة الإرهاب	counter terrorism
إجراءات وقائية	preventive measures
أعلن الحرب على	to declare war on
تبنّى الإرهاب	to sponsor terrorism
متبنّي الإرهاب	sponsor of terrorism
إرهاب صادر عن الدولة	state-sponsored terrorism
هجوم إرهابي	terrorist attack
حدث إرهابي، أحداث إرهابية	terrorist incident
تهديد إرهابي	terrorist threat
اكتشاف تهديدات	threat detection
عرقل شبكة إرهابية	to disrupt a terrorist network
مسهّل شبكة	network facilitator
جماعات إرهابية	terrorist groups
كادر، كوادر	cadre
خلية، خلايا	cell

منظّمة إرهابية	terrorist organisation
تنظيم إرهابي	"
حرّم	to proscribe (e.g. an organisation)
محرّم	proscribed
قائمة مراقبة	watch list
القاعدة	Al-Qa'ida
القيادة المركزية	central leadership
أوى يَأوي إرهابياً (إيواء)	to harbour a terrorist
تهريب إرهابي	terrorist trafficking
دليل إرهابي، دلائل إرهابية	terrorist handbook
طريقة عمل	modus operandi
معسكر تدريب	training camp
تجذَّر	radicalisation
دعاية	propaganda
حملة دعائية	propaganda campaign
إضفاء الشرعية على العنف	legitimation of violence
إرهابي	terrorist

مخرّب	saboteur/terrorist
عمليات تخريبية	sabotage operations
أعمال تخريبية	terrorist acts
قام يقوم بأعمال تخريب (قيام)	to commit sabotage
تخطيط تنفيذي	operational planning
تخطيط العمليات	operations planning
مهمّة	mission/assignment
مهمّة تقصّي الحقائق	fact-finding mission
اغتيال	assassination
محاولة اغتيال	assassination attempt
اغتيال موجّه	targeted assassination
قاتل	assassin/hitman
مرتزق، مرتزقة	mercenary
هدف سهل	soft target
هدف محصّن	hard target
هدف تصادفي	target of opportunity
هدف عالي القيمة	high-value target
أستُشهد	to die/be martyred
شهيد، شهداء	dead person (martyr)

خاطف \ مختطف	kidnapper
خاطف طائرات	hijacker
رهينة، رهائن	hostage
أخذ يأخُذ رهينة (أخْذ)	to take hostage
حاجز الرهائن	hostage taker
أزمة الرهائن	hostage crisis
كبير المفاوضين حول الرهائن	chief hostage negotiator
متطلبات المختطفين	kidnappers' demands
فدية	ransom
فدية نقدية	cash ransom
طالب بفدية	to demand a ransom
احتجز رهينة	to hold to ransom
فكّ الرهائن	hostage release
قطع الرأس	beheading
انفجار	explosion
متفجّرات	explosives
متفجّرات بلاستيكية	plastic explosives
تفجّر	to erupt/explode (intransitive)

فجّر	to explode (transitive)
كرّاسة صنع قنابل	bomb-making manual
دليل صنع قنابل	"
مادّة صنع قنابل	bomb-making materials
صاعق	detonator
مفجّر	"
سيّارة مفخّخة	car bomb
قنبلة موقّتة	time bomb
رسالة ملغّمة	letter bomb
تفخيخ	booby trap
هجوم انتحاري	suicide attack
هجوم استشهادي	"
جهاز متفجّر مرتجل	improvised explosive device (IED)
عبوة حارقة	incendiary device
قنبلة محرقة	"
بيت آمن	safe house
منزل آمن	"

مخبأ أسلحة	arms cache
متمرّد	rebel/insurgent
مقاومة التمرّد	counter insurgency
محارب \ مقاتل \ مناضل	militant
مجموعة فدائية	militant group/ guerrilla group

9. HUMAN INTELLIGENCE

جاسوس، جواسيس	spy
تجسّس	espionage/spying
مكافحة الجاسوسية	counter espionage
حلقة تجسّس	spy ring
سحق يسحَق شبكة تجسّس (سَحْق)	to crack a spy network
شغّل جواسيس	to run spies
مرشد جواسيس	spymaster
عقل موجّه	mastermind
نظّم	to mastermind
متحكّم	controller
مرؤوس	subordinate
عميل، عملاء	agent
عميل مزدوج	double agent
خائن	defector
عميل محرّض	agent provocateur
منفّذ	operative

عنصر، عناصر	operative/member (of organisation)
تعاون	to collaborate
متعاون	collaborator
واشٍ	informer/stool pigeon
مخبر \ مبلّغ	informant
تسرّب معلومات	leak of information
حذّر	to tip off
وسيط، وسطاء	intermediary/ go-between
مصدر استخباراتي	intelligence source
طوّر العلاقات مع مصدر	to cultivate a source
جنّد	to recruit
استهدف للتجنيد	to target for recruitment
تقدير نفسي	psychological assessment
جرّم	to incriminate
فضح يفضَح (فَضْح)	to expose/ compromise
ورّط	to implicate

ابتزاز	blackmail/extortion
أجبر على	to force (into doing)
مكيدة	entrapment
عملية فخّ	sting operation
مخادعة	subterfuge
خداع	deception
محاولة تغطية	attempted cover up
ستار دخاني	smoke screen
إيجاز	briefing
استجواب	debriefing
ملتقى	rendezvous
اتّصل ب	to make contact with
نقطة الرسائل الميّتة	dead letter/drop box
فريق مراقبة	surveillance team
مراقبة مضادّة	counter surveillance
راقب تلفوناً	to tap a telephone
كشك هاتف	telephone box/booth
تلصّص	to bug
كاشف تلصّص	bug detector/sweeper

جهاز إنصات	bug/listening device
تلصّص في الوقت الحقيقي	live tapping
حدّد جهاز إرسال	to locate a transmitter
دسّ ميكروفون	to plant a microphone
كلام خفي	veiled language
كلام حذر	guarded speech
حبر سرّي	secret ink/ invisible ink
ميكروفيلم	microfilm
مكشاف الكذب	polygraph/ lie-detector
مرآة ثنائية الاتّجاه	two-way mirror
مرآة تفتيش	inspection mirror
أثبت شخصيته	to identify oneself
تعرّف على	to identify
بطاقة هوية	ID card
لوحة الرقم	number plate/ licence plate
مولد	place of birth
تاريخ الميلاد	date of birth

تحت ستار	under cover
قصّة ستار	cover story
ستار عميق	deep cover
تحت اسم مستعار	incognito
شبكة سرّية	clandestine network
عملية خاصّة	special operation
فريق عمليات	operations team
فريق حماية	protection team
دفاع ذاتي	self defence
حارس، حرّاس	bodyguard/sentry
حرس	bodyguard (unit)
مدرّع	armour-plated
سيّارة مدرّعة	armoured car
زجاج مضادّ للرصاص	bullet-proof glass
سترة مضادّة للرصاص	bullet-proof vest
كاتم الصوت	silencer (gun)
عازل للصوت	soundproof
سمّ	poison
سيانيد	cyanide

جهاز تنفّس	aqualung
عدائي	hostile
متسلّل	plant/infiltrator
تسلّل	to infiltrate
تسرّب	"
اخترق	to penetrate
خطوط التسلّل	infiltration routes
منفذ الدخول والخروج	entry and exit point
دخيل، دخلاء	intruder
سلك شائك	barbed wire
نظام إنذار	alarm system
عبِث يعبَث ب (عَبَث)	to tamper with
فتح يفتَح قفل بآلة مدبّبة (فَتح)	to pick (a lock)
قفل أرقام	combination lock

10. COMMUNICATIONS TECHNOLOGY

استخبارات الإشارات	signals intelligence (SIGINT)
استطلاع إلكتروني	electronic intelligence (ELINT)
استخبارات الاتّصالات	communications intelligence
اتّصالات \ مواصلات	communications/telecommunications
قانون الاتّصالات	telecommunications law
بنية الاتّصالات العالمية	global communications infrastructure
اتّصالات فضائية	satellite communications
مواصلات لاسلكية	radio/wireless communications
التقط	to intercept (communications)
موقع التقاط	intercept site
رصيف التقاط	intercept platform

تتبّع	to track
نشاط الهدف	target activity
على مدى البصر	line-of-sight
انتشار	propagation
خطّ سلكي	landline
خطّ أرضي	"
سمع تلفوني	wire tapping
خطّ الاتّصال بالأقمار الصناعية	satellite uplink
خطّ التوصيل من الأقمار الصناعية	satellite downlink
ميكرووييف	microwave
متعدّد القنوات	multichannel
قناة لاسلكية	channel (radio/wireless)
عامل لاسلكي	radio operator
جهاز تحويل لاسلكي	radio-relay equipment
محطّة تقوية	booster station
عريض النطاق	wideband

ضيّق النطاق	narrowband
مسح يمسَح (مَسْح)	to scan/sweep
تردّد المسح	scan frequency
تردّد راديوي	radio frequency
تردّد واطئ	low frequency
تردّد عالٍ	high frequency (HF)
تردّد عالٍ جدّاً	very high frequency (VHF)
تردّد عالٍ مفرط	ultra high frequency (UHF)
تعديل التردّد	frequency shift
نقل التردّد	"
توليف	tuning
تماثلي	analogue
مستقبل	receiver
جهاز استقبال	"
هوائي	antenna/aerial
هاتف مؤمّن	secure telephone
نغمة الاتّصال	dialling tone

خطّ ساخن	hot line
تحويلة	telephone extension
دليل هاتف	telephone directory
رمز الاتّصال الهاتفي	dialling code
لوحة مفاتيح	keyboard/telephone switchboard
خطّ خاصّ	dedicated line
مشترك	subscriber
جهاز محمول يدوياً	handheld device
هاتف يدوي	handset
جوّال \ هاتف جوّال	cell phone/mobile phone
شريحة، شرائح	Subscriber Identity Module (SIM) card
شوّش	to jam (e.g. radio)
جهاز مضادّ للتشويش	anti-jamming device
تشويش لاسلكي	radio jamming/radio interference
استقبال لاسلكي	radio reception
شبكة واسعة	wide area network (WAN)

شبكة المنطقة المحلّية	local area network (LAN)
قوّة الإشارة	signal strength
منطقة التغطية	footprint (e.g. communications)

11. INFORMATION TECHNOLOGY

تكنولوجيا المعلومات	information technology (IT)
معلوماتية	information technology (IT)/ informatics
أحدث التكنولوجيات	state-of-the-art technology
حافة أمامية	leading edge
بنية نهاية إلى نهاية	end-to-end architecture
بنية النظم	systems architecture
قاعدة الاتّصال، قواعد الاتّصال	(internet) protocol
مهندس النظم	systems engineer
تحليل النظم	systems analysis
دليل الأساليب	systems manual
نظام المعلومات	information system
استرجاع المعلومات	information retrieval

computerisation/ computing	حوسبة
mainframe computer	حاسبة إطارية
neuro-computers	حاسبات عصبية
backbone	الأعمال الرئيسية
server	حاسوب الخدمة
computer operator	مشغّل كمبيوتر
work station	محطّة عمل
desktop services	خدمات سطح المكتب
technical support	دعم فنّي
computer processing	تشغيل
central processing unit (CPU)	وحدة تشغيل مركزية
real time processing	معالجة في الوقت الحقيقي
"	تحليل في الوقت الحقيقي
data processing	معالجة البيانات
database	قاعدة البيانات
database management	إدارة قواعد البيانات
data exchange	تبادل البيانات

تخزين البيانات	data storage
جهاز تخزين	storage device
وسيطة، وسائط لتخزين البيانات	storage media
وسائط قابلة للاستبدال	removable media
قرص مدمج	compact disc (CD)
بطاقة ذكية	smart card
جهاز خرج	output device
وحدة تشغيل الأقراص	disk drive
قرص صلب	hard disk/hard drive
بريد إلكتروني	e-mail
وصلة بيانات	data link
إرسال بيانات رقمية	digital data transmission
شبكات رقمية	digital networks
إشارة رقمية	digital signal
تبديل حزمي	packet-switching
توجيه	routing/forwarding
باندوذ مفتوح	unlimited bandwidth

(systems) audit/auditing	تدقيق الحسابات
audit trail	سجلّ مراجعة
error detection	اكتشاف الخطأ
error recovery	استخلاص الخطأ
data sampling rate	معدّل أخذ عيّنات البيانات
data dictionary	معجم البيانات
algorithm	خوارزمية
recursive algorithm	خوارزم تكراري
programming languages	لغات برمجة

12. INFORMATION SECURITY

أمن المعلومات	information security
تأمين المعلومات	information assurance
أمن المواصلات	communications security (Comsec)
متحذِّر من أمن المواصلات	Comsec aware
صمت لاسلكي	radio silence
اتّصالات محدودة	restricted communications
اتّصالات مقيَّدة	"
شبكة مواصلات	communications network
انقطاع المواصلات	disruption of communications
مخاطر معلوماتية	information risk
تقدير الأخطار	risk assessment
إدارة المخاطر	risk management
تحليل الخطر	risk analysis
تحليل التأثير	impact analysis

معيار تقييم الأمن، معايير تقييم الأمن	security evaluation criterion
أدوات التقييم	evaluation tools
مستوى التأمين	assurance level
اعتماد	accreditation
اعتمادية الخدمة	reliability of service
علبة مضادّة للتلاعب	tamper-proof casing
قابلية للتأثر	vulnerability
ضعف قابل للاستغلال	exploitable vulnerability
احتياطي	back-up (e.g. communications)
أرشيف احتياطي	back-up archive
إسهاب شبكي	network redundancy
الانترنت	cyber/the Internet
عالم الانترنت	cyberspace
الدفاع عن الانترنت	cyber defence
هجوم عبر الانترنت	cyber attack
تهديد من الانترنت	cyber threat

متخصّص في أمن الانترنت	cyber security specialist
جريمة عبر الانترنت	cybercrime/e-crime
ملكية فكرية	intellectual property
نمو الانترنت	growth of the internet
قرصنة (على) الانترنت	internet piracy
مزوّر	pirated
اختراق \ تهكير	hacking
متسلّل \ هكر	hacker
اختبار الاختراق	penetration testing
هجوم إلكتروني	electronic attack
محاولة تداول	access attempt
أسلوب تداول	access mode
كود التداول	access code
مراقبة الدخول	access control
كاسر	anonymiser
اتّصل	to log on
اتّصال عن بعد	remote log-on
انقطع	to log off

log-off	انقطاع
to run/execute a programme	شغّل برنامج
executable (e.g. file)	قابل للتشغيل
active file	ملفّ فعّال
denial of service	نفي الخدمة
to power down (e.g. computer)	توقّف
to disrupt (e.g. system)	عرقل
disruption of service	عرقلة الخدمة
to disable (e.g. computer)	عطّل
to patch	رقّع
patching	ترقيع
network defence	دفاع شبكي
network analysis	تحليل شبكي
computer network exploitation	استغلال شبكة الكمبيوتر
integrated network operations	عمليات الانترنت المتكاملة

رموز حاسب	computer code
نظام العدّ الثنائي	binary code
جهاز متوافق مع الحاسب	cloned computer
هندسة معكوسة	reverse engineering
أمن التحقّق	verification security
التحقّق من الهوية	user authentication
توقيع إلكتروني	electronic signature
امتياز	authorisation
ميزات إدارية	administrative privileges
معرّف	username
رقم سرّي	pin number
كلمة السرّ	password
كلمة المرور	"
كلمة المرور المشفّر	enciphered password
دفتر عناوين، دفاتر عناوين	address book
اسم مستعار	alias
هوية كاذبة	false identity
اسم المجال	domain name

حاسوب خدمة بروكسي	proxy server
استضافة	hosting
جدار ناري	firewall
حجب يحجُب (حَجْب)	to block
ثغرة	gap/breach
إعادة التوجيه	redirect
نصّب	to install
برنامج مبني، برامج مبنية	firmware
برمجيات مشتركة	shareware
نزّل	to download
تنزيل	download (-ing)
حمّل	to upload
تحميل	upload (-ing)
ابلود	"
أعدى حاسبة	to infect a computer
برنامج خبيث	malware
مبرمج البرامج الخبيثة	malware programmer
أزال البرامج الخبيثة	to remove malware
فيروس	virus

Trojan	برنامج حصان طروادة
worm attack	هجوم دودة
botnet attack	هجوم برنامج آلي على الانترنت
"	هجوم بوتنت
backdoor attack	برنامج اختراق الحاسبة
"	برنامج التسلّل
rogue programme	برنامج مخداع
rogue operator	مشغّل مخادع
internet cookies	ملفّات الارتباط
spam	سبام
spam message	بريد مزعج
software error	خطأ برمجيات
anti-virus software	برنامج ضدّ الفيروسات

13. INTELLIGENCE ANALYSIS

حلّل	to analyse
تحليل المخابرات	intelligence analysis
محلّل استخبارات	intelligence analyst
تحليل الهدف	target analysis
اكتشاف أهداف	target discovery
تحليل الأحداث	events analysis
تحليل الشبكات الاجتماعية	social network analysis
تحليلات مدمجة	fused analysis
تقارير مدمجة	fused reporting
استنبط	to extrapolate
افترض	to hypothesise
فرضية	hypothesis
استنتج	to infer/deduce
استخلص	to deduce
رياضيات	mathematics

تشفير	encryption
تشفير لا متناظر	public key encryption
مرفق المفاتيح العمومية	public key infrastructure
شفرة \ شيفرة	cipher
شفرة \ شيفرة	code
كلمة رمزية	codeword
اسم رمزي	codename
خريطة شيفرة	cipher chart
مشفّر \ شفري \ كودي	in cipher/ enciphered/ encrypted
رسالة رمزية	encoded message
برقية رمزية	enciphered telegram
حلّ، يحُلّ (حَلّ)	to decipher
حلّ الرموز \ حلّ الشفرة	to decode
فكّ يفُكّ الرموز (فَكّ)	to crack the code
كود مورس \ إشارات مورس	Morse code
خريطة تحويل	conversion chart
برنامج الجدولة	spreadsheet

حروف اختصار	acronym
صيغة، صيغ	format
مصفوفة	matrix
تحليل مصفوفي	matrix analysis
كلمة مفتاح	keyword
كلمة دليلية	"
سماعة رأس	headphones
خصائص الصوت	voice characteristics
نسخ ينسَخ (نَسْخ)	to transcribe
نسخة	transcript
ترجم	to translate/interpret
ترجمة	translation
مترجم	translator/interpreter
خدمات ترجمة	translation services
قاموس لغة أجنبية، قواميس لغة أجنبية	foreign language dictionary
مسرد مصطلحات	glossary of terms
دليل متخصّص	specialist directory
معجم جغرافي	gazetteer

خطّ العرض	latitude
خطّ الطول	longitude
تحديد الموقع الجغرافي	geolocation
نظام تحديد الموقع العالمي	global positioning system (GPS)
تحديد الاتّجاه	direction finding
إعداد الخرائط	mapping
أداة رسم الخرائط	mapping tool

INDEX

abuse, to (one's authority) *see* to exceed/abuse (one's authority)
access
    access attempt, 75
    access code, 75
    access control, 75
    access mode, 75
accountability, 9
accreditation, 74
acquisition range, 42
acronym, 82
activate/initialise, to, 8
    to activate (the alarm), 8
active file, 76
address book, 77
administrative privileges, 77
aerial *see* antenna
aerial reconnaissance, 41
aerospace defence, 33
agent, 57
    agent provocateur, 57
    blister agent, 37
    double agent, 57
    incapacitating agent, 37
    nerve agent, 37
    riot control agent, 49
air-launched cruise missile, 42
alarm system, 62
alert status, 6
    on full alert, 6

algorithm, 72
    recursive algorithm, 72
alias, 77
Al-Qa'ida, 52
alternative energy, 27
Amnesty International, 26
analogue, 65
analyse, to, 80
    events analysis, 80
    fused analysis, 80
    impact analysis, 73
    intelligence analysis, 80
    intelligence analyst, 80
    matrix analysis, 82
    risk analysis, 73
    systems analysis, 69
    target analysis, 80
anarchy, 17
anonymiser, 75
antenna/aerial, 65
anti-jamming device, 66
anti-semitism, 17
anti-virus software, 79
aqualung, 62
Arab League, 25
    Arab League General Secretariat, 25
Arab nationalism, 18
Arab Spring, 21
area of responsibility, 8

armed conflict, 39
Armed Forces Chief of Staff, 39
armed guard, 49
armour
    armoured car, 61
    armour-plated, 61
    body armour, 49
arms
    arms cache, 56
    arms control, 31
    Arms Control and Disarmament Agency, 26
    arms inspector, 33
    arms race, 31
    disarmament, 31
    firearm, 50
ARRC (Advanced Rapid Reaction Corps), 39
arrest warrant, 47
arsenal, 39
ASEAN (Association of South-East Asian Nations), 26
assassin/hitman, 53
    assassination, 53
    assassination attempt, 53
    targeted assassination, 53
assignment *see* mission
assurance level, 74
asylum seeker, 15
atomic mass, 34
attempted cover up, 59
audit trail, 72
audit/auditing (systems), 72
authentic documents, 47

authorisation, 77
authoritarianism, 18
authority
    coalition provisional authority, 19
    to exceed/abuse (one's authority), 19
    to impose authority, 18
autocracy, 19
available energy, 27
AWACS (airborne warning and control system), 41
    AWACS aircraft, 41
axis of evil, 13
axis powers, 13

backbone, 70
backdoor attack, 79
background radiation, 35
back-up (e.g. communications), 74
    back-up archive, 74
bacteria, 36
bail
    he was released on bail, 48
    to jump bail, 48
ballistics, 33
    ballistic missile defence system, 31
    inter-continental ballistic missile, 33
    short-range ballistic missile, 33
barbed wire, 62
baton/truncheon, 49
BDA (battle damage assessment), 42
beacon *see* homing device
beheading, 54

binary code, 77
biological reconnaissance system, 36
biometrics, 14
blackmail/extortion, 59
blister agent, 37
block, to, 78
body armour, 49
bodyguard (unit), 61
bodyguard/sentry, 61
bomb
    bomb-making manual, 55
    bomb-making materials, 55
    car bomb, 55
    letter bomb, 55
    precision bombing, 42
    time bomb, 55
booby trap, 55
booster station, 64
border
    border control, 14
    Border Guard, 14
    border police, 14
    border security forces, 14
    cross-border operation, 15
botnet attack, 79
breach *see* gap
bribery/bribe, 47
briefing, 59
    debriefing, 59
buffer zone, 43
bug/listening device, 60
    bug detector/sweeper, 59
    to bug, 59
bullet-proof glass, 61
bullet-proof vest, 61

bureau of investigation, 25
    to call in the Federal Bureau of Investigation (FBI), 25

cadre, 51
call in, to (the FBI), 25
camera
    concealed camera, 8
    X-ray pulse camera, 8
car bomb, 55
caretaker government *see* interim government
cargo
    high-interest cargo, 15
    illicit cargo, 15
cash ransom, 54
CCTV (closed circuit television), 8
CD (compact disc), 71
cell, 51, 66
cell phone/mobile phone, 66
central leadership, 52
centrifuge, 34
chaff rockets, 43
chain of command, 39
chain reaction, 35
channel (radio/wireless), 64
check list, 46
check, to (up on), 46
checkpoint, 14
checks and balances, 45
chief hostage negotiator, 54
Chief of Staff, Operations, 39
CIA (Central Intelligence Agency), 25

cipher, 81
　cipher chart, 81
　enciphered password, 77
　enciphered telegram, 81
　in cipher/ enciphered/ encrypted, 81
　to decipher, 81
civil defence, 6
civil liberties, 16
civil war, 21
clandestine network, 61
classification
　classification chart, 10
　security classification/ protective marking, 10
classified documents, 10
clean *see* not under suspicion
cleanup, 36
climate change, 28
cloned computer, 77
clue *see* lead/clue/ evidence
coalition forces, 39
coalition provisional authority, 19
code, 81
　codename, 81
　codeword, 81
　encoded message, 81
　Morse code, 81
　to decode, 81
Cold War rivalry, 13
collaborator, 58
　to collaborate, 58
collective security, 5
colonialism, 19
combat readiness, 40

combating climate change, 28
combination lock, 62
command and control (C2), 39
　command and control centre, 39
commando, 40
commit, to (an offence), 48
commit, to (genocide), 16
commit, to (sabotage), 53
communication
　communication channels, 7
　communications centre, 7
　communications intelligence, 63
　communications network, 73
　communications/ telecommunications, 63
　Comsec (communications security), 73
　Comsec aware, 73
　disruption of communications, 73
　global communications infrastructure, 63
　radio/wireless communications, 63
　restricted communications, 73
　satellite communications, 63

telecommunications law, 63
compartment, to (e.g. information), 9
compliance with procedure, 9
comprehensive test-ban treaty, 32
compromise, to *see* to expose
computer
   cloned computer, 77
   computer code, 77
   computer network exploitation, 76
   computer operator, 70
   computer processing, 70
   computerisation/ computing, 70
   mainframe computer, 70
   neuro-computers, 70
Comsec aware, 73
concealed camera, 8
confidence-building measures, 21
confidentiality, 10
constitute, to (a threat), 7
constitutional law, 21
constitutional monarchy, 21
containment device, 36
control of the straits, 20
controlled substances, 32
controller, 57
conventional energy sources, 27
conversion chart, 81
cooperative defence initiative, 13
cordon, 50
   to cordon off an area, 50
corporate security policy, 9
counter espionage, 57
counter insurgency, 56
counter narcotics, 14
counter proliferation, 31
counter surveillance, 59
counter terrorism, 51
coup/coup d'état/ upheaval, 21
court
   appeal court, 48
   court martial/ military court, 48
   court of inquiry, 48
   ICJ (International Court of Justice), 26
   to refer a dispute to the international court, 16
   to take to court, 48
cover story, 61
   deep cover, 61
   under cover, 61
covert operation, 40
CPU (central processing unit), 70
crack, to (a spy network), 57
crackdown/repression, 19
crime
   crimes against humanity, 16
   detection and prevention of serious crime, 5

transnational organised crime, 15
war crimes, 16
critical
   Critical National Infrastructure, 27
   critical phase, 7
   critical situation, 7
   time-critical, 7
cross-border operation, 15
crude oil, 28
cult of personality, 19
cultivate, to (a source), 58
curfew, 19
custody, in, 47
customs, 14
   customs control, 14
cyanide, 61
cyber
   cyber attack, 74
   cyber defence, 74
   cyber security specialist, 75
   cyber threat, 74
   cyber/the Internet, 74
   cybercrime/e-crime, 75
   cyberspace, 74

data
   data dictionary, 72
   data exchange, 70
   data link, 71
   data processing, 70
   data protection, 10
   data sampling rate, 72
   data storage, 71
   database, 70
   database management, 70
   digital data transmission, 71
date of birth, 60
dead letter/drop box, 59
debriefing, 59
deception, 59
decipher, to, 81
declare, to (a state of emergency), 6
declare, to (war on), 51
decode, to, 81
decommission, to, 36
dedicated line, 66
deduce, to, 80
deep cover, 61
defector, 57
defence
   aerospace defence, 33
   ballistic missile defence system, 31
   biological defence programme, 36
   civil defence, 6
   cooperative defence initiative, 13
   cyber defence, 74
   defence technology, 39
   network defence, 76
   nuclear-biological-chemical defence, 31
   self defence, 61
   Strategic Defence Initiative, 31
demand, to (a ransom), 54
democratisation, 20
demographic change, 22

demographic explosion, 22
demonstrations, 49
denial of service, 76
depleted uranium, 34
depoliticise, to, 21
desktop services, 70
detained, 47
detection and prevention of serious crime, 5
detective, 46
detention centre, 49
   provisional detention, 49
deterrent forces, 32
detonator, 55
dialling code, 66
dialling tone, 65
dictatorship, 19
die/be martyred, to, 53
digital data transmission, 71
digital networks, 71
digital signal, 71
diplomatic bag, 14
diplomatic channels, 13
diplomatic immunity, 13
direct exposure, 35
direction finding, 83
disable, to (e.g. computer), 76
disarmament, 31
disk drive, 71
dispersion, 36
disrupt
   disruption of communications, 73
   disruption of service, 76
   to disrupt (a terrorist network), 51
   to disrupt (e.g. system), 76
dissenter, 21
disturbances *see* riots
doctrine (to follow a), 17
document
   authentic documents, 47
   classified documents, 10
   forged documents, 47
   official documents, 10
   technical documents branch, 10
   to guard a document, 10
   travel documents, 10
   unclassified documents, 10
dogma, 17
   dogmatism, 17
domain name, 77
double standards, 21
download (-ing), 78
   to download, 78
drone *see* UAV (unmanned aerial vehicle)
drop box *see* dead letter
drug dealer, 15
   drug trafficking, 14
DV (developed vetting), 10

early warning radar, 42
economic diversification, 27
economic stability, 5

economic wellbeing, 5
e-crime *see* cybercrime
electromagnetic pulse, 40
electronic
   electronic attack, 75
   electronic counter measures, 43
   electronic intelligence (ELINT), 63
   electronic signature, 77
   electronic warfare, 40
e-mail, 71
emergency
   emergency decontamination, 36
   emergency evacuation, 6
   emergency plan, 6
   state of emergency, 22
   to declare a state of emergency, 6
enciphered password, 77
enciphered telegram, 81
encoded message, 81
encryption, 81
   public key encryption, 81
end-to-end architecture, 69
energy, 27
   alternative energy, 27
   available energy, 27
   conventional energy sources, 27
   energy conservation, 27
   energy efficiency, 27
   offshore energy, 27
enforce, to (security), 9
entrapment, 59

entry and exit point, 62,
environmental disaster, 29
environmental protection, 5
error detection, 72
error recovery, 72
erupt, to, 54
espionage/spying, 57
ethnic cleansing, 16
ethnic minority, 18
EU (European Union), 26
European convention on extradition, 16
European Court of Justice, 26
evaluation tools, 74
events analysis, 80
evidence *see* lead/clue/evidence
exceed/abuse, to (one's authority), 19
executable (e.g. file), 76
execute, to (a programme) *see* to run (a programme)
explode, to (intransitive) *see* to erupt
explode, to (transitive), 55
exploitable vulnerability, 74
exploration (oil), 28
   to explore (for oil), 28
explosion, 54
explosives, 54
   IED (improvised explosive device), 55
   plastic explosives, 54
export controlled information, 32

expose/compromise, to, 58
extortion *see* blackmail
extradition, 15, 16
   European convention on extradition, 16
   extraditable offence, 15
   extradition treaty, 16
   extraordinary rendition, 15
   to fight extradition, 15
   to hand over (e.g. for extradition), 16
extraordinary rendition, 15
extrapolate, to, 80
extremism, 17
   extremist, 17
eye scan, 14

fact-finding, 46, 53
   fact-finding mission, 53
false identity, 77
fight, to (extradition), 15
fine, 48
   to fine/impose a fine, 49
fingerprinting, 14
firearm, 50
firewall, 78
firmware, 78
fissile material, 34
follow up/pursuit, 46
   to follow up, 46
follow, to (a doctrine), 17
footprint (e.g. communications), 67

force
   border security forces, 14
   coalition forces, 39
   deterrent forces, 32
   force multiplier, 39
   joint task force, 8
   peacekeeping forces, 16
   special forces, 40
   task force, 8
   to force (into doing), 59
   use of force, 39
foreign language dictionary, 82
forged documents, 47
format, 82
forwarding *see* routing
fraud squad, 47
free and fair elections, 20
freeze on settlements, 20
freeze, to (oil prices), 28
frequency
   frequency shift, 65
   HF (high frequency), 65
   low frequency, 65
   radio frequency, 65
   scan frequency, 65
   UHF (ultra high frequency), 65
   VHF (very high frequency), 65
full alert, on, 6
fundamentalism, 17
   fundamentalist, 17
fused analysis, 80
fused reporting, 80

gamma ray, 35
gap/breach, 78
gas
    gas detector, 37
    gas mask, 37
    mustard gas, 37
gather, to (intelligence), 6
gazetteer, 82
GCC (Gulf Cooperation Council), 25
general amnesty, 21
Geneva Convention, 26
geolocation, 83
germ warfare, 36
global communications infrastructure, 63
global security, 13
glossary of terms, 82
go-between *see* intermediary
Golan Heights, 20
GPS (global positioning system), 83
gross violation, 17
ground control, 7
growth of the internet, 75
guard, to (a document), 10
guidance system, 33

hacker, 75
    hacking, 75
hand over, to (e.g. for extradition), 16
handcuffs, 50
handheld device, 66
handling of confidential information, 10
handset, 66
harbour, to (a terrorist), 52

hard disk/hard drive, 71
hard target, 53
headphones, 82
hearing *see* trial
heightened security measures/procedures, 9
high frequency (HF), 65
high threat area, 35
high-interest cargo, 15
highly enriched uranium, 34
high-value target, 53
hijacker, 54
hitman *see* assassin
hold, to (to ransom), 54
homing device/beacon, 42
hostage, 54
    chief hostage negotiator, 54
    hostage crisis, 54
    hostage release, 54
    hostage taker, 54
    to take hostage, 54
hostile, 62
hosting, 78
hot line, 66
human rights, 16
    Human Rights Act, 16
    human rights activist, 16
human trafficking, 15
humanitarian crisis, 16
hypothesis, 80
    to hypothesise, 80

IAEA (International Atomic Energy Agency), 24

IAEA safeguards, 32
ICC (International Criminal Court), 26
ICJ (International Court of Justice), 26
ID card, 60
identification system, 42
    IFF (identification friend or foe), 42
identify, to, 60
identify, to (oneself), 60
IED (improvised explosive device), 55
illegal immigrant, 15
    illegal immigration, 15
illicit cargo, 15
illumination radar, 42
immediate threat, 7
impact analysis, 73
implicate, to, 58
impose, to (authority), 18
incapacitating agent, 37
incendiary device, 55
incite, to, 49
incognito, 61
incriminate, to, 58
incursion, 20
indictment, 48
infect, to (a computer), 78
infer/deduce, to, 80
infidel, 18
infiltrate, to, 62
    infiltration routes, 62
    infiltrator *see* plant
informant, 58
    informer/stool pigeon, 58

informatics *see* IT (information technology)
information
    handling of confidential information, 10
    information assurance, 73
    information retrieval, 69
    information risk, 73
    information security, 73
    information system, 69
    IT (information technology), 69
    leak of information, 58
    restricted information, 9
    to compartment (e.g. information), 9
    to withhold information, 46
infra-red detector, 40
initialise, to *see* to activate
inspect, to, 33
    inspection mirror, 60
    inspections regime, 32
install, to, 78
institutional change, 19
insurgent *see* rebel
integrated network operations, 76
intellectual property, 75, 57

intelligence
  CIA (Central Intelligence Agency), 25
  communications intelligence, 63
  ELINT (electronic intelligence), 63
  House Intelligence Committee, 24
  IC (the intelligence community), 24
  intelligence (e.g. reports), 6
  intelligence (organisation), 5
  intelligence analysis, 80
  intelligence analyst, 80
  intelligence apparatus, 24
  intelligence directorate, 24
  intelligence source, 58
  Joint Intelligence Committee, 24
  Ministry of Intelligence, 24
  operational intelligence, 6
  Senate Intelligence Committee, 24
  SIGINT (signals intelligence), 63
  strategic air intelligence, 6
  to gather intelligence, 6
intercept, to (communications), 63
  intercept platform, 63
  intercept site, 63
inter-continental ballistic missile, 33
interim/caretaker government, 19
international narcotics control board, 15
internet
  cyber/the internet, 74
  growth of the internet, 75
  internet cookies, 79
  internet piracy, 75
  internet police, 45
  internet protocol, 69
  see also cyber
interpret, to *see* translation
interrogate/question, to, 46
intifada *see* uprising
intruder, 62
investigation, 46
  independent investigation, 46
  investigation is requested (into), 46
  investigatory powers, 46
  money-laundering investigation, 47
  police investigator, 46
  to investigate, 46
  to launch a criminal investigation, 46
Islamic Salvation Front, 25
isotope separation, 34

jam, to (e.g. radio), 66
   anti-jamming device, 66
   radio jamming/radio interference, 66
Joint Intelligence Committee, 24
joint task force, 8

keyboard/telephone switchboard, 66
keyword, 82
kidnapper, 54
   kidnappers' demands, 54

LAN (local area network), 67
landline, 64
laser, 40
latitude, 83
launch, to (a criminal investigation), 46
launch/mount, to (an operation), 40
law
   constitutional law, 21
   law enforcement agency, 45
   law enforcement forces, 45
   martial law, 19
   rule of law, 17
   to maintain law and order, 45
lead/clue/evidence, 47
leading edge, 69
leak of information, 58
legitimisation of violence, 52
letter bomb, 55

liaison officer, 13
licence plate *see* number plate
lie-detector *see* polygraph
life prison sentence, 49
line-of-sight, 64
liquid missile propellant, 33
live tapping, 60
locate, to (a transmitter), 60
lock, to (onto a target), 42
log off, to, 75
   log-off, 76
log on, to, 75
   remote log-on, 75
longitude, 83
low frequency, 65

main supply route, 32
mainframe computer, 70
maintain, to (law and order), 45
make, to (contact with), 59
malfunction, 6
malware, 78
   malware programmer, 78
   to remove malware, 78
manoeuvres *see* military exercises
mapping, 83
   mapping tool, 83
martial law, 19
martyr *see* die/be martyred, to
mass unemployment, 22
mastermind
   to mastermind, 57

mathematics, 80
matrix, 82
   matrix analysis, 82
member (of organisation) *see* operative
MEPP (Middle East Peace Process), 20
mercenary, 53
metropolitan police, 45
microfilm, 60
microwave, 40, 64
   microwave bombardment, 40
militant, 56
military exercises/manoeuvres, 39
military police, 45
mindset, 8
Ministry of Information, 24
Ministry of Intelligence, 24
Ministry of the Interior, 24
minority
   ethnic minority, 18
   minority faction, 18
   minority rule, 18
   Sunni/Shi'a majority/minority, 18
missile
   air-launched cruise missile, 42
   ballistic missile defence system, 31
   inter-continental ballistic missile, 33
   liquid missile propellant, 33
   Missile Technology Control Regime, 32
   short-range ballistic missile, 33
mission/assignment, 53
   fact-finding mission, 53
mobile *see* cell phone
modus operandi, 52
money-laundering investigation, 47
monitoring system, 32
Morse code, 81
mount, to (an operation) *see* to launch (an operation)
mounted police, 45
multichannel, 64
multi-disciplinary approach, 8
multi-purpose, 8
Muslim Brotherhood, 25
mustard gas, 37

narcotics, 14
   counter narcotics, 14
   international narcotics control board, 15
   see also drug
narrowband, 65
national
   Arab nationalism, 18
   Critical National Infrastructure, 27
   National Guard, 18
   national security, 5
   National Security Advisor, 24
   National Security Council, 24
   national security threat, 5

national unity government, 18
NATO (North Atlantic Treaty Organization), 26
navigation system, 41
navy reconnaissance plane, 41
need-to-know basis, on a, 9
neo-Nazi, 17
nerve agent, 37
network
    computer network exploitation, 76
    integrated network operations, 76
    network analysis, 76, 80
    network defence, 76
    network facilitator, 51
    network redundancy, 74
neuro-computers, 70
neutral territory *see* no man's land
Nile water agreement, 29
no-fly zone, 16
nuclear
    nuclear deterrent, 31
    nuclear device, 35
    nuclear fission, 34
    nuclear non-proliferation treaty, 32
    nuclear power industry, 31
    nuclear proliferation, 31
    nuclear reaction, 35
    nuclear reactor, 35
    nuclear stockpile, 31
    nuclear-biological-chemical defence, 31
    nuclear-free zone, 32
    thermo-nuclear warhead, 33
number plate/licence plate, 60

OAU (Organization of African Unity), 26
occupation, 20
Occupied Territories, the, 20
offence
    extraditable offence, 15
    to charge with a criminal offence, 48
    to commit an offence, 48
official documents, 10
offshore energy, 27
OIC (Organization of the Islamic Conference), 25
oil
    crude oil, 28
    oil exploration, 28
    oil fields, 28
    oil production, 28
    oil refinery, 28
    oil refining, 28
    oil wealth, 28
    oil well, 28
    OPEC (Organization of the Petroleum Exporting Countries), 28

proven oil reserves, 28
to explore for oil, 28
to freeze oil prices, 28
operation
   Chief of Staff, Operations, 39
   covert operation, 40
   cross-border operation, 15
   integrated network operations, 76
   operational intelligence, 6
   operational planning, 53
   operational readiness, 40
   operations planning, 53
   operations team, 61
   special operation, 61
   sting operation, 59
   to launch/mount an operation, 40
operative/member (of organisation), 57, 58
oppositionist, 21
output device, 71
outstation, 8
overthrow, to (the regime), 21

packet-switching, 71
paper shredder, 11
particle, 36
   particle beam weapon, 36
passenger screening, 14
passive sonar *see* active/passive sonar

password, 77
patching, 76
   to patch, 76
payload, 33
peacekeeping forces, 16
penetrate, to, 62
   penetration testing, 75
photographic reconnaissance, 41
physical security, 5
pick, to (a lock), 62
pin number, 77
pirated, 75
place of birth, 60
plague, 36
plant, to (a microphone), 60
plant/infiltrator, 62
plastic explosives, 54
PLO (Palestine Liberation Organization), 25
poison, 61
police
   border police, 14
   internet police, 45
   metropolitan police, 45
   military police, 45
   mounted police, 45
   police chief, 45
   police investigator, 46
   police officer, 45
   police post, 45
   police state, 19
   riot police, 49
   to obstruct the police, 45
political
   political activist, 17
   political anarchy, 17

political Islam, 17
political refugee, 20
polling station, 20
polygraph/lie-detector, 60
power
   axis powers, 13
   power base, 13
   power grid, 27
   power of attorney, 45
   power station, 27
   superpowers, 13
   to power down (e.g. computer), 76
   transfer of power, 19
precision bombing, 42
preventive, 6, 34, 51
   preventive action, 34
   preventive measures, 51
principles of the UN Charter, 23
priority, 5
prison cell, 49
probation period, 48
   on probation, 48
programming languages, 72
prohibited activities, 47
prohibited items/materials, 9
prohibited zone, 9
propaganda, 52
   propaganda campaign, 52
propagation, 64
proportionality, 9
proscribed, 52
   to proscribe (e.g. an organisation), 52
protection shelter, 37
protection team, 61
protective action, 34
protective custody, 49
protective marking/security classification, 10
protective suit, 37
protectorate, 19
protester, 22
protocol (internet), 69
proven oil reserves, 28
proxy server, 78
psychological assessment, 58
psychological warfare, 40
public key encryption, 81
   public key infrastructure, 81
pursuit *see* follow up

question, to *see* to interrogate

racism, 18
   racist, 18
radar
   early warning radar, 42
   fire control radar, 42
   illumination radar, 42
   radar coverage, 42
   radar cross section, 42
radiation
   acute radiation dose, 35
   background radiation, 35
   radiation detection instrument, 34
   radiation dispersal weapon, 36

radiation protection
  instruments, 34
radiation sickness, 35
radical, 17
  radicalisation, 52
  radicalism, 17
radio
  radio/wireless
    communications, 63
  radio frequency, 65
  radio jamming/radio
    interference, 66
  radio operator, 64
  radio reception, 66
  radio silence, 73
  radio-relay equipment, 64
radioactive
  radioactive decay, 35
  radioactive
    decontamination, 36
  radioactive fallout, 35
  radioactive half-life, 35
radiological
  radiological
    protection, 34
  radiological release, 34
  radiological sabotage, 35
  radiological warfare, 34
ransom, 54
  cash ransom, 54
  to demand a ransom, 54
  to hold to ransom, 54
reactionary, 19

reactor core meltdown, 35
readiness status, 40
  combat readiness, 40
  operational readiness, 40
real time processing, 70
rebel/insurgent, 56
receiver, 65
reconnaissance
  aerial reconnaissance, 41
  biological reconnaissance system, 36
  navy reconnaissance plane, 41
  photographic reconnaissance, 41
  reconnaissance aircraft, 41
  satellite reconnaissance, 41
  see also surveillance
reconstruction, 20
recruit, to, 58
  to target for recruitment, 58
recursive algorithm, 72
Red Crescent, 25
redirect, 78
re-entry vehicle, 33
refer, to (a dispute to the international court), 16
refugee resettlement, 20
  political refugee, 20
regime
  inspections regime, 32
  regime change, 19
  regime stability, 5
  sanctions regime, 16

released on bail, 48
relevant authorities, the, 7
reliability of service, 74
remand
    on remand, 48
    remand centre, 48
    to remand in custody, 49
    to remand on bail, 48
remote control, 33
    remote log-on, 75
    remote sensor, 33
removable media, 71
remove, to (malware), 78
rendezvous, 59
reporting channels, 7
repression *see* crackdown
resistance/staying power, 22
resources, 27
restricted area, 9
restricted communications, 73
restricted information, 9
reverse engineering, 77
revolution, 21
revolutions per minute (rpm), 34
Richter scale, 35
right-wing organisation, 17
riot, 49
    riot control agent, 49
    riot gear, 49
    riot police, 49
risk analysis, 73
risk assessment, 73
risk management, 73
rogue operator, 79
rogue programme, 79
Rome Treaty, 26
routing/forwarding, 71
rule of law, 17
ruling family, 21
run, to (spies), 57
run/execute, to (a programme), 76

sabotage operations, 53
saboteur/terrorist, 53
safe house, 55
safety, 6
sanctions regime, 16
satellite
    satellite communications, 63
    satellite downlink, 64
    satellite uplink, 64
scan
    eye scan, 14
    scan frequency, 65
    scanner, 14
    to scan/sweep, 65
screener/screening officer, 14
    passenger screening, 14
search warrant, 47
secessionist, 22
secret, 10, 60
    secret ink/invisible ink, 60
    top secret, 10
Secretary General, 25
sectarianism, 18
secure telephone, 65
security
    border security forces, 14
    collective security, 5

Comsec (communications security), 73
corporate security policy, 9
cyber security specialist, 75
global security, 13
heightened security measures/ procedures, 9
information security, 73
national security, 5
National Security Advisor, 24
National Security Council, 24
national security threat, 5
physical security, 5
security belt, 13
security breach, 9
security clampdown, 19
security classification/ protective marking, 10
security clearance, 10
security counter measures, 9
security dossier/file, 11
security evaluation criterion, 74
security forces, 13
security integration, 13
security requirements, 5
security shield, 5
security situation, 7
security studies, 5
security-conscious, 9
to enforce security, 9
UNSC (United Nations Security Council), 23
verification security, 77
sedition, 49
self defence, 61
Senate Intelligence Committee, 24
sentry *see* bodyguard
separatist, 22
serve, to (a warrant), 47
server, 70
sever, to (diplomatic relations), 13
shareware, 78
Shi'a majority/minority *see* Sunni/Shi'a majority/minority
shock wave, 35
short notice, 7
short-range ballistic missile, 33
shred, to (paper), 11
signal strength, 67
signals intelligence (SIGINT), 63
silencer (gun), 61
situation report (sitrep), 42
situation room, 7
situational awareness, 42
smart card, 71
smart weapons, 42
smoke bomb, 50
smoke screen, 59

smuggling
: human trafficking, 15
: terrorist trafficking, 52
: weapons smuggling, 15

soft target, 53
software error, 79
solid fuel, 33
sonar *see* active/passive sonar
soundproof, 61
spam, 79
: spam message, 79

special forces, 40
special operation, 61
specialist directory, 82
sponsor of terrorism, 51
: state-sponsored terrorism, 51
: to sponsor terrorism, 51

spreadsheet, 81
spy, 57
: counter espionage, 57
: spy ring, 57
: spying *see* espionage
: spymaster, 57
: to crack a spy network, 57
: to run spies, 57

stabilised situation, 7
standard operating procedure, 40
state of emergency, 22
state-of-the-art technology, 69
state-sponsored terrorism, 51
station chief, 8
staying power *see* resistance
step-by-step reduction, 32
sting operation, 59
stockpile, to, 31
stool pigeon *see* informant
storage device, 71
storage media, 71
storm troops, 40
storm, to, 40
strait jacket, 50
Strait of Hormuz, 20
Straits of Gibraltar, 20
strategic air intelligence, 6
Strategic Defence Initiative, 31
strategic importance, 13
stun grenade, 50
stun gun, 50
subordinate, 57
subscriber, 66
: SIM (Subscriber Identity Module) card, 66

subterfuge, 59
Suez crisis, 20
suicide attack, 55
Sunni/Shi'a majority/minority, 18
supply, 27, 32
: supply chain, 32

supporting documents, 46
surveillance
: counter surveillance, 59
: surveillance aircraft, 41
: surveillance platform, 41

surveillance system, 41
surveillance team, 59
see also reconnaissance
survival technology, 37
suspect *see* under suspicion
sustainable development, 28
sweep, to *see* to scan
sweeper *see* bug detector
system
    alarm system, 62
    AWACS (airborne warning and control system), 41
    ballistic missile defence system, 31
    biological reconnaissance system, 36
    GPS (global positioning system), 83
    guidance system, 33
    identification system, 42
    information system, 69
    monitoring system, 32
    navigation system, 41
    surveillance system, 41
    systems analysis, 69
    systems architecture, 69
    systems audit/auditing, 72
    systems engineer, 69
    systems manual, 69

tail, to *see* to track/trace/run a trace/tail
take, to (to court), 48
tamper, to (with), 62
    tamper-proof casing, 74
tap, to (a telephone), 59
target
    hard target, 53
    high-value target, 53
    soft target, 53
    target activity, 64
    target analysis, 80
    target discovery, 80
    target of opportunity, 53
    to lock onto a target, 42
    to target for recruitment, 58
targeted assassination, 53
task force, 8
tear gas, 49, 50
    tear gas grenade, 50
technical documents branch, 10
technical support, 70
technology transfer, 32
telecommunications *see* communications
telecommunications law, 63
telemetry, 33
telephone
    secure telephone, 65
    telephone box/booth, 59
    telephone directory, 66
    telephone extension, 66

telephone switchboard *see* keyboard
terrorism
    counter terrorism, 51
    sponsor of terrorism, 51
    state-sponsored terrorism, 51
    terrorist, 51, 52, 53
    terrorist acts, 53
    terrorist attack, 51
    terrorist groups, 51
    terrorist handbook, 52
    terrorist incident, 51
    terrorist organisation, 52
    terrorist threat, 51
    terrorist trafficking, 52
    to disrupt a terrorist network, 51
    to harbour a terrorist, 52
    war on terror, 51
thermo-nuclear warhead, 33
think tank, 8
threat
    cyber threat, 74
    high threat area, 35
    immediate threat, 7
    national security threat, 5
    terrorist threat, 51
    threat detection, 51
    threat of force, 7
    threat reduction, 7
    threat state, 6
    to constitute a threat, 7
time bomb, 55

time-critical, 7
tip off, to, 58
totalitarianism, 18
trace, to *see* to track/trace/run a trace/tail
track, to, 47, 64
track/trace/run a trace/tail, to, 47
training camp, 52
transcribe, to, 82
transcript, 82
transfer of power, 19
translation, 1, 82
    to translate/interpret, 82
    translation services, 82
    translator/interpreter, 82
transnational organised crime, 15
transparency, 10
transport of hazardous waste, 36
travel advice, 14
travel documents, 10
trial/hearing, 48
    on trial, 48
tribalism, 18
Trojan, 79
truncheon *see* baton
tuning, 65
two-way mirror, 60

UAV (unmanned aerial vehicle)/ drone, 41
ultra high frequency (UHF), 65

UN (United Nations)
   principles of the UN Charter, 23
   UN Charter, 23
   UN Interim Force, 23
   UN mission, 23
   UN observers, 23
   UNESCO (UN Educational, Scientific and Cultural Organization), 23
   UNGA (UN General Assembly), 23
   UNRWA (UN Relief and Works Agency), 23
   UNSC (United Nations Security Council), 23
   UNSCOM (UN Special Commission), 23
   UNSCR (UN Security Council Resolution), 23
unclassified documents, 10
under cover, 61
under suspicion/suspect, 47
   not under suspicion (clean), 47
unlimited bandwidth, 71
upheaval *see* coup/coup d'état
upload (-ing), 78
   to upload, 78
uprising, 21
uprising/(Palestinian) intifada, 21
use of force, 39

user authentication, 77
username, 77

veiled language, 60
verification security, 77
very high frequency (VHF), 65
Vienna Convention, 26
virtual team, 8
virus, 78
vital installation, 27
voice characteristics, 82
vulnerability, 74
   exploitable vulnerability, 74

WAN (wide area network), 66
war
   civil war, 21
   Cold War rivalry, 13
   electronic warfare, 40
   germ warfare, 36
   psychological warfare, 40
   radiological warfare, 34
   to declare war on, 51
   war crimes, 16
   war on terror, 51
   warhead, 33
warrant, 47
   arrest warrant, 47
   search warrant, 47
   to serve a warrant, 47
watch list, 52
water cannon, 50
water shortage, 29
weapon
   particle beam weapon, 36

radiation dispersal
    weapon, 36
smart weapons, 42
weapons smuggling,
    15
weapons transfer, 32
WMD (weapons of
    mass destruction),
    31
West Bank, 20
whistle blower, 11
wideband, 64

wire tapping, 64
wireless communications
    see radio/wireless
    communications
work station, 70
worm attack, 79
worst-case scenario, 35

X-ray pulse camera, 8

Zionism, 18
    Zionist, 18